Redshift

1

© 2018 Respective Writers

All rights reserved for the author.
Please contact the author for permissions.

Arroyo Seco Press

Redshift Anthology #1

www.arroyosecopress.org

logo by Morgan G. Robles
morganrobles.carbonmade.com

ISBN-13: 978-1-7326911-0-0
ISBN-10: 1-7326911-0-X

for Michelle

Poems

Crossing the Desert 1
River Rats 2
Songs of Spring 3
take back 4
i lose 5
the show 6
lover's dilemma 7
Polaris 8
Where I live 9
Application 10
Fear 11
Tornadoes and Debris 13
Residuum 15
Garden Comfort 17
When Dreams Die 18
Demon in a Bottle 19
How to Save a Jaguar 20
The First Time I Felt Rain 21
Frontiers 22
Travelers 24
Cold Confetti 26
Just Space 27
Apple-Headed 29
outside a bar called hemingway's 30
My Memory 31
If Only 33
Soothsayer 34
His Weekend of Dark and Light 35
Rune 1: Taken Daily 36
Rune 5: Plea from a Future Educator 37
My Daydream 38
Ode to the Guitar Player 39
this is me calling 40
Lies, All Lies 41
Gloomy Sunday 45
The Strawberry Field 47
I can taste the ash 51
Prima Facie 52
Expect Delays 53
The First Time Again 57
I was texting 58
Letter to a Shipwreck 59
Morgue-hardened 60
Premonition of Descent 61
California Summer 2018 62
Memories of Eldorado 63
Civilization 64
Buddy 65
Jonah Brushing His Hair 67

In the Dirt and Dead Leaves 68
The Beggar Becomes Chewser 70
Reciprocate and Replicate 72
Ford Flex 73
Balcony 74
Landline 75
Highwire 77
Couplets Written in the Dark In Search of Home 78
old crows 79
-- .. - - - - - - . . . . (Morse code "Zombies") 80
Sleep 81
Charlie Parker 82
May Crowning 83
Grandma's House 84
Landscape Photographer Wanted 85
Melania 86
That Great Big Beautiful Bastard 88
The Feral Children of Los Angeles 90
Dear Wisconsinites 94
Letter to an Old Flame: The Upstairs Lounge 96
Somewhere Over the Darkened 97
Eating A Slug In Germany 98
After Hours 100
The Eulogists 101
Batboy Escapes! 102
Cheshire Cat 103
Condolence Card 104
On the Way to JFK 105
His Armor 106
Off the Trail in Joshua Tree 107
The Death in the Large Family: Part 1 108
Obituary: The Sequel 111
Sunshine: Final 113
Fate Ignores My Resolve 115
Dreams of Falling 116
Water Witch 117
For Rosa 118
Atomic Spaces 120
Better Worlds 121
Amor de Madre 122
My Mother's Perfume 123
Brian's Late Funeral 124
The Desert; a Love in Pictures 125
Beau 127

Redshift

the expanding universe
always shifting from the earth
as if we were focal

Michelle Thomas

Crossing the Desert

Four o'clock in the early morning.
Quick bowl of cereal,
cool, crisp desert air.
Watching my parents
fill up the radiator bag with water.

Worry and stress in their voices.
Loving every moment of our new adventure.
Key in, engine turns over.
Yeah!

Every stop, my parents check the radiator bag.
Is it full, cool enough?
How is the radiator doing?
Will we make it?

Michelle Thomas

River Rats

I remember beady eyes,
Hisses, long sharp teeth
jumping towards me.

Utter fear and the screams
River Rats, the demons
of the rat world.
Huge as cats,
not cuddly at all,
but MONSTERS.

Michelle Thomas

Songs of Spring

Mockingbirds' scales of melodic songs.
Baby birds' raw caws of hunger.
A few chirps, quietness!
Leaves rustling as the parents
hunt for food for the babies.

Kitty Anarchy

take back
all the
stuff i know
now

i'd rather
go back
to being happy

Kitty Anarchy

i lose
far many more
things
than you've
given me

Kitty Anarchy

the show

lies and fake smiles
are the lubrication
needed to function
in this fake society

no one is prepared
to handle the truth
they would crumble
at one honest word
that didn't feed their ego

Kitty Anarchy

lover's dilemma

no respect
no relationship

when we say no
the stakes
are suddenly raised

hostages
to their
rage

lovers
turn into
beaters
stalkers
killers

then they
wonder why
we stay

Lloyd David Aquino

Polaris

He wants to ask her about the cobwebs clinging to the steering wheel that embarrass his fingers into making promises. Headlights blossom wanderlust fireflies. Shine the sticky sweet off loose change. Tumbleweed of torn nylons

She's an hour coming, red-blooded, pumps worrying strip mall veins. A patrol car lullabies a recently widowed gas station. Grasshoppers are intoxicated and eloping behind chainlink fences.

He watches her undress a bottle. Crumple a brown bag to panties to fling past his ear. Christen the rain-spotted roof with black liquor. Broken glass silences his shoes.

Why do I let you take me anywhere I know, he says?

She says, If I were the North Star, you wouldn't ask me that.

Nail polish blushes. They twirl together under nervous streetlight. Shoulder painting shoulder. The stoplights try on three shades of makeup, three shades of makeup, three shades. The gutters soak in orange cat lapping up gutter.

Lloyd David Aquino

Where I live

A streetlight loves its own shadow.
Sidewalk can never make up its mind.
Fences are ashamed.
Cul-de-sacs cut themselves for attention.

I live where the grass can't afford the mortgage.
Sometimes the trains never crash.
Sometimes the helicopters find religion.
I live close enough to hear the freeways beg for change.

A mailbox nurses a broken heart.
Trees complain of arthritis from too much love-making.
Doorways will let anyone inside them.
No one knows a sprinkler by its real name.

This house and I were conceived the same day in January.
Neighborhoods were still on speaking terms.
The manure stunk of the Cold War.
Everyone stole cable.

Rooftops drink alone.
Windows shudder at the sight of themselves.
No one carries torches anymore.
No one visits porches anymore.

Lloyd David Aquino

Application

She submits
the forms in black
ink not blue like her mother
taught her under the ceiling
fan and over the table

the tip of her
pen tearing across
each piece of paper
and the little
bones in her
wrist and hand
remember

every movement
a recitation
how to spell
yes I exist but this
is not me this is
only temporary I only
need to survive this
month don't turn this
around I can turn this
around
without needing
to start all over

Lorraine Biteranta

Fear

Do you remember that night?
A party not too long ago
Drinking and dancing and
Just going with the flow

Perhaps you may remember
At the party that one night
Your sweaty body dancing
My clothes on way too tight

Do you remember this?
A drink from you to me
Filled with drugs and horrors
Of the night that was to be

Do you remember now?
Or at least the spot in back
Where you dragged my drugged up body
And started the attack?

Do you remember it?
You ignored my weakened pleas
You pushed inside and grunted
left a tremble in my knees.

Do you remember well?
You left me all alone
In a giant shed too injured
to find my way back home.

I hope that you remember
Because I cannot forget
My mind replays a movie
Of this night that I regret.

Lorraine Biteranta

You should remember well
Because the next time we embrace
I'll see that fear will register
Upon your dark, sadistic face

For I'll sneak into your bedroom
And crawl into your bed
Images of foul play
Will race inside your head

And when the timing comes
And when the hour's right
I'll ask if you remember me
From the party that one night

And I'll see the recognition,
The growing, trembling fear
Your bedroom should be haven
But now your nightmare's here.

You'll lie and say it wasn't you
That we have never met
But through your panicked lying
My intentions have been set.

I'll watch the fear spread
I'll see it in your eyes
I'll pull the metal trigger
And silence those crass lies.

And when my task is finished
After which I will be free
I'll know at least one new thing:
You do remember me.

Lorraine Biteranta

Tornadoes and Debris

To notice me
is to notice a tornado.
Fascinating, unique,
overbearing.

To notice me
means to run,
to hide away
and hope I won't reach you.

To watch me
is to watch a withered tree.
To witness all the sun's beauty
shining down
and acknowledging
only death and decay.

To watch me
means to cringe,
knowing I, too
was beautiful once,
but now eyes need time
to look away.

Lorraine Biteranta

To love me
is to love a brand new house
for shelter it provides
and comfort that you seek
to love me
is to watch that house decay
to grow tired
and resent the way I'm built.

To love me
is to walk away
before I crumble to debris
at your feet.

Lorraine Biteranta

Residuum

Remember the day you handed him
that brown box filled with tabs and tabs
of acid? When you told him to take a tab
onto his tongue and he told you
"no?"

Remember when you told him
"man up, no son of mine
is going to get his panties in a bunch
over drugs. Stop being a pussy,
stick it in your mouth."

And those are the same words
you used when you creeped
into my bedroom,
no shirt on no shoes no socks
no pants no boxers
nothing, nothing on

and you remember how you told me
"stick it in your mouth, whore.
I am not here to play father
but you better believe
it when I say that I am your daddy"
And do you remember that day

that he overdosed? And that day
that acid turned into heroin turned
into cocaine turned into a hospital
and rehab and a jail cell and that day

Lorraine Biteranta

turned into me
packing my stuff, running away
living homeless,
alone.

That day you were released from jail
after serving only a few months

was the worst day of my life.

Francesca Borella

Garden Comfort

Rich, ebony soil and
Musky, damp fragrance of Mother Earth
Reaches into my soul
And soothes my aches of life.
I long to lie on the ground
And feel her warm embrace,
The kind that only a mother can give
To her child.

Francesca Borella

When Dreams Die

I used to dream lusty dreams,
Of being held close to naked skin.
Hands cupped my head
And lips brushed across my neck,
Finally finding firm connection on my own.
I used to feel his breath on my goose-bumped arms
And taste salty sweat as our body movement intensified.
Then calm and satisfied after each night encounter,
I dreamed it would all become real.

It's been years since I had that dream.
Oh yes, I long for that passion we used to share,
Deep in my thoughts, only in my mind.
Today, my old school logical brain
Tells me to give it up.
No one would want a gray wrinkled hag.
Who would waste their time?
So, my fantasy has faded and weeks go by.
I'm all alone now on dreamless nights, with an empty mind.

Francesca Borella

Demon in a Bottle

I try to get beyond the memory
Of your vodka breath.
I want to think that the times you forgot
To pick me up from after school,
You were work exhausted and not
Passed out from being drunk.
I still remember that time
You wouldn't look at my new college degree,
Directing my attention to the cat instead,
It was because you had tears of pride in your eyes.
I know you loved me,
And with your anguished soul,
You couldn't show me that you cared.
You left me so many years ago and yet
Still, I wait to hear it.

Francesca Borella

How to Save a Jaguar

The old jaguar was sprawled out
Comfortable of the bluff.
He saw us in our riverboat, but he didn't care.
His scarred face and graying fur
Told me this was nothing new for him.
I worried about the impact
Of so many ecotourists looking
and trying to get a glimpse.
Then, it occurred to me this was a better fate
Than being hunted for his fur
or having his land stolen away.

Scott Noon Creley

The First Time I Felt Rain

It tapped a hushed staccato beat on the brim of my yellow plastic hat as I bent over to watch the water sluice away the earth. The ground disappeared like a magic trick, there and gone – what seemed to be solid retreating to reveal the still-bright colors of a buried toy robot. I remember how the ground still boiled and heaved, no longer a fixed thing, and it was all suddenly so alien. Just four years old, I felt like an astronaut, an archaeologist. I wanted to plunge my hands into the earth and find what I was sure must lay deeper – the bones of the child who had owned the toy robot, the boy who had lived here first. I needed to find him. I needed to sing him a lullaby, to read him *Good Night Moon*. Anything to spare him the blade of the rain. I looked at the rain-blurred silhouette of my mother in the kitchen, the light pouring around her in a fuzzy nimbus. I prayed he had someone like her, someone to tuck him back to the warm, dry bed of the earth and dark.

Scott Noon Creley

Frontiers

I'm flying over a broken, arctic ice field
and leaning over the porthole.
"We're between Russia and Alaska,"
I tell Samm, my former student,
"this is where Viktor catches up with The Creature."
We stare at the endless, fractured patchwork below us,
she doesn't answer.

"He freezes up here," I say,
but I don't specify whether it's Victor or The Creature,
creator of created, who dies.

The ice cap below us must be massive
because I'm thirty thousand feet in the air,
and I can still see the silver cracks and valleys
in it.

The sun is metallic and alien in the broad mirror of the glacier.
I've been told that this ice is one of our main cosmic defenses –
and that this ice is melting.

The windows in the Air China plane are magic.
When you touch a button it floods with visible azure gas.
It filters the light, turns everything in the plane
the same dreamy sky blue.

Scott Noon Creley

I've learned to say thank you in Chinese.
I whisper it to the vanishing ice –
"Xièxiè,"
I say to the array of crystallized water molecules,
thousands of feet below;
A brief "thank you" for
the plate armor come jewelry as it slowly heats
and liquefies, changes states. Retreats.

Through the window,
I see the polar ice-caps blunting the roaring,
pyroclastic sunlight, all that heat and death and life
both particle and wave, photosynthesis fuel and cancer.
I imagine it sending that flood of light ricocheting back
out into the greater, endless darkness of space,
what the Chinese call "the up-and-out"
back where there are celestial bodies fencing in the chaos.
the earth is preserving us,
its little accidents via further accidents –

The interior of the plane is so dim.
Samm's face is stained blue by the window shade.
Looking at that light as it roars back into space,
I think that every noble act
is really just thermodynamics,
every saint just mere universal law in motion –
an accident –

But accidents are everything.

Scott Noon Creley

Travelers

That night,
several hours after we've left the Yi Village,
the bus full of my students slows down.
The police have partially-blocked the road
where a car has gone into the ditch,
where it still lies face down, crumpled,
now something discarded.

I see a lumpy shape
sprawled across our lane,
and, instinctually, I stand up,
the sharp panic of mortality
ripping a jagged path down my spine.
I shout at my students –
"Don't look!"
They do, of course, look.
We all look.

The dead businessman
on the side of the road
is the color of parchment,
the dull, shallow kind of hue
one might expect from a mineral,
but not from skin.
Dried blood splatters his face,
has left runnels down his chin,
has painted his shirt like wine stains –
As if he'd drunk recklessly from deep, wide cup
and was now insensate on the side of the road.

Scott Noon Creley

After we pass,
we're all silent.
We keep traveling
in the direction the dead man was traveling,
alongside the thousands of other cars
who cut across the farmland and endless countryside
as if forming a train of lanterns
a caravan to guide each other through the night.

Eventually, the lights of Kunming
Fill the horizon,
a bright, guileless, kaleidoscopic smear
against the overwhelming dark.
It all suddenly looks so noble.
As if the luminescence-wreathed buildings and signs
are a bulwark,
a burning picket line
arrayed against
the smog-wreathed inevitability of night.
A line of calligraphy every city forms,
a defiant line of poetry written together against
the great barrier we must all eventually scale.

Scott Noon Creley

Cold Confetti

The glossy plastic had shattered like hard candy.
It mixed in with the leaves and grass on the freeway divider
cold confetti as distant and inappropriate
as the numb heat of my fingertips,
when I trailed them down the fragile architecture of your spine,
and told you that I had just wanted to do something
that could never be undone.

Larry Duncan

Just Space

The roots took the foundation first.
Once the concrete cracked,
it didn't take long for the walls
to warp, and bring the roof down.
After that, the old garage
gave its secrets like charity.
Magazines and unopened letters
spilled out in the lawn,
and were crushed to pulp under
the sneakers of curious teens.
It was their rocks that finished the windows.

Let the radio remember
the words we promised to forget.
We can sing the long day
about the hands that cut and suture,
knock once and fall away.
Father's long fingers at work
binding the feather to the hook,
his careful plotting of lures
leaving little question which fish would drown.

Even after he died,
Mother stayed in the kitchen,
her hands on the roller,
working the dough flat.
Every morning, she showed us how to cut.
"The saw has its place,"
said Frigidaire and Kenmore.
"Just like teeth in a kiss."

Larry Duncan

The band has brought the trumpets.
It seems like a strange day for a parade,
but I can hear them in the dust
cloud down the road.
They call the graves to turn,
every Sunday we buried
opening its face to blister.

I see you have taken the attic as home.
I am no longer allowed in the house.
I live in the leaves now,
in the thin bodies of insects.
Come down, brother.
The ladder is at the window,
and the weather is fine.
I've a fresh pack a gum,
and a secret to share.
There were never walls here.
We were never born.
The sun told me so.
I stared at it all day.
It left circles in my eyes.

Larry Duncan

Apple-Headed

My dog hunts old bones.
Withered to a stick,
all I am counts hours
by the ridges of his spine.

Hours in delirium,
hours in spite,
hours ecstatic and unraveled
in the tremolo of his whine.

"Do you see,"
ask his ramble ribs.
"Do you sea?
Do you abc…?
Do you hear the thimble
roar of the spindle unwind?
Or is it just water in your ear?"

All I answer is bottle.
The day left to dwindle,
like salt to a snail,
in the wake of whiskey burn.
I don't dare arrange the letters,
let alone rise and leave the porch.

He runs a ragged line along the fence,
nosing the earth for holes.
There are none, but he searches.
He's caught a scent.

There's digging to be done,
and I will have to answer
the hollowness of what
he lays at my feet.

Larry Duncan

**outside a bar called hemingway's a
decade or so into the new millenium**

Hello?
Are you there?
Or is this the message?
I'm on my way to thank you,
but the power has failed.
I may not make it home tonight.
It's breaking up.
My battery is failing.
The lights are all out,
and the traffic is revolving.
I think it might be the lines,
a surge in the current.
Everything is dark here
except for the signals.
The wind has them spinning,
every one flashing red.

The tremors are long overdue.
Mounds of crushed glass and stone
will welcome us tomorrow.
I can see the corners now,
where the homeless sleep,
all the open doors
that lead to a few laughs.
I'll be pulling onto your tongue any minute.
The rest is history, in fashion or not.

So, goodnight.
I love you.
Tell the kids,
the broken places
are pretty in the light.

Barbara Eknoian

My Memory

Once, my memory was sharp as a silver blade.
I could play guessing actors'
and actresses' names by their initials.
Now, I watch TV and I say,
Oh, that's the actor who was in that movie.
You know the war one with that blonde guy.
Or, remember that's the actress
who made love to that foreign actor.
She's the one who had the affair
with that big Italian movie star.
You know the one who I mean, right?

Once, I could think back and name
families who lived in my friend's
HUD apartments
more than sixty years ago
because I used to play there:
The Della Donnas were on the first floor,
right across the hall from The Murrays,
The Knapps lived on the second floor,
and my best friend, Mary Dorrity
lived across the hall from them.
The Fletchers lived on the top floor
across from one of my playmates,
but now I can't think of her name.

Barbara Eknoian

Recently, I was at my fiction class
and I wanted to address one
of the five members. I almost panicked
because I couldn't think of her name,
and she's the hostess.
Sorry, I explain. *For some reason
I'm losing names even though
I know who you are.*

Now, whenever I leave my driveway,
I pause and ask myself,
Where are you going? If I don't ask,
who knows where my car might take me?
I'm a writer, who fears losing words.
How will I remember which one to choose,
if I can't even rely on a dictionary
because I can't recall the word?
You know what I mean. Don't cha?

Barbara Eknoian

If Only
   For my brother, Livio

*Tie a yellow ribbon
round the old oak tree,*
Tony Orlando sings
at the Golden Nugget.
The older crowd is up
and out of their seats
clapping and singing along.
Orlando jokes, *Thank God,
they remember the words.*
The small band sounds
fill the room:
two electric guitars,
two keyboards, and drums.
The strobe lights caress
the band members' shoulders
as they play.

I'm mesmerized watching
the lights flit around the stage
When the drummer
is spotlighted,
 I see you instead:
Your strong hands strike
the cymbals, your head bobs
with the beat.
My eyes well up with tears.
I think *if only, if only.*
You could've been that drummer
with the band bringing
a room full of old-timers
to their feet once more,
inspiring them to sing
all the way home.

Barbara Eknoian

Soothsayer

O to have been a fortune teller
dressed in a purple caftan
with a fuchsia scarf
tied around my head.
I'd reach out and turn over the palm
of my oldest brother's hand
telling him, Don't let marijuana
and boozy barroom women
beguile you. You'll be crushed
as though a boa constrictor
were squeezing out your life.

I'd look into the future
and warn my middle brother,
Don't go out to sea.
The merchant seamen are rougher
than waves crashing over
the smoke stack in a hurricane.
Your artist's eye and poet's mind
will come back forever altered
by the ugly banter of men
in need of a woman's touch,
and you'll emerge dressed in silk
and satin longing for softness.

For the youngest brother,
I'd spread the cards before me
as though playing solitaire, warning,
Heroin will take you from moments
of bliss to a lifetime of hell.
Run from it, don't turn around,
or you'll turn into a pillar of salt.

Barbara Eknoian

His Weekend of Dark and Light

Just suppose you are the cashier
who assumes this poorly dressed person
is homeless, so you chase him
from your restaurant
and refuse to let him use the restroom.
His feelings are hurt and he sits
beside the building sobbing.

Maybe, the next day you are the one
who thinks he is staring at your girlfriend.
You punch him in the nose
and make him bleed.
He's so shocked he calls the police,
but they judge him by his clothing,
ignore his complaint against the hitter,
and drive him to his sister's house
He cries, "I don't get any respect."

On Sunday, you might be the drummer
playing on the boardwalk at Venice Beach.
When he walks by, and asks if he can have
a turn at your drums, you let him.
Afterwards his heavy frame feels lighter.
His mood has turned to sunshine.
He says, "This was one of my best days."

Now the cashier, the jealous boyfriend,
and the drummer are not aware
he was so depressed
that he died on Monday.
Be careful about what you put out
into the universe.
Choose light!

Jeffrey Graessley

Rune 1: Taken Daily

with the ease of stripping
bark
from tree-trunks—the depths

of depression can be answered
in flood
      all the carried baggage
      of a short or long
      lifetime

will rise in audience
made powerless
and cast away—Geirroth shoving Agnar
          back to sea.

teach me, Gelding and Father

to find safety
under this shade,

the etchings to move
mountains—or simply

rise
from bed
in the morning.

Jeffrey Graessley

Rune 5: Plea from a Future Educator

teach me
that perfect counter,

Ultimate Defense

the words
    to stop the spray

bump-stocked rifles
in measured hands

(a simulation of full auto)

that have already marked
me short

      my body
  can only cover
so many.

Sarah Gurney

My Daydream

I travel on my bicycle,
The breeze and sun on my face.
A shaft of light
Comes out from the dark
Across the teal blue water.

I hit the brakes.
I've just come out from my own sense of dark
As the wind blows through my hair,
And I feel strange light on my face.

Colored lights flash before me,
My reflection in the water.
I dismount as the wind stops
Faster than the speed of dark.

Before I know it, those lights are gone.
A new breeze whips my hair
When I look at the water.
I return to my bicycle
As light fades.

When I closely look at the moonlight,
I no longer feel that I am in the dark.
I pedal away, with the moon on one side of my face.
The moon shines across the invisible water.
I catch a glimpse of you
From the shadow of my bicycle.

Your hair is just as dark,
Compared to the moonlight reflecting off the glint in your eyes.
I turn away from the water and ride away.

I realize now that I will never see you again.
Whenever I look up at the sky,
I will always see your face in the moonlight.

Sarah Gurney

Ode to the Guitar Player

I think you want me.
Screaming like a runaway train,
    Your guitar is like a heartbeat.
I want to jump inside your body
    And reside in the fingers you set the strings on.

I shouldn't be watching you,
    But I can't help it.

You cradle your instrument
    Like a lover does after a one-night stand.

My resistance flakes away
    Like rust off an old Central Pacific boxcar.

I know what I like,
And what I like wants me.

Sarah Gurney

this is me calling

i want to talk about foreign affairs and affairs of the heart and news around the world and generation x and classic movies and classic rock and what to buy my mother for christmas and if i should buy the newest iPhone and what to tell me what i should do with my life tomorrow the next week the next year or the next decade i want to talk about how i should think of the people around me and how they are lost in a maze and why i feel i am the only one who feels the way i do-that everything happens for a reason i want to talk about a room with a view and why i am not ready to die and why i am not afraid of living i want to talk about how i should just run along the shore screaming at the top of my lungs that i am free and why it is all right to color outside the lines and what i should wear for the next fifty years and i don't care what people are saying about the newest anything and other recent trends

also, i want to put in a good word for the trees

Curtis Hayes

Lies, All Lies

in a film history class
the teacher would sometimes
veer off from the importance of Pasolini
or the arrogance of John Ford
and roll on about his days
as a TV writer,
especially his time on
the 70's investigative series,
In Search Of.
I loved *In Search Of*
the way every twelve-year-old
loved Bigfoot and the Bermuda Triangle
and the Roswell UFO crash.
I believed in Spontaneous Human Combustion.
every week Leonard Nimoy hosted.
he would tell us about something inexplicable
in his slow, familiar voice,
sometimes raising an eyebrow as he
recited a particularly disturbing fact.
when the teacher told us that
almost all of the episodes were bullshit,
that he and the other writers
had made most of it up
typing their lies right up to
the moment cameras rolled,
I was crushed.

Curtis Hayes

Vulcans don't lie
I had trusted Nimoy
to report only
the most thoroughly investigated
natural mysteries
and paranormal phenomenon.
after that class
I couldn't believe anything.

a few years later
I was working at NBC
wrapping a stage with the crew at the end of
another chaotic day on set.
the important people were all gone
so the music was turned up.
after a few tracks the long strings intro
to Barry White's "Can't Get Enough of Your Love Babe"
wound through the cavernous room.
"Oh yeah" I said mostly to myself.
a few feet away, one of the guys was wrangling C-stands.
he gave me a small nod,
"My uncle Irwin played violin on some of these records."
I froze.

Curtis Hayes

"Wait. Your uncle was in the Love Unlimited Orchestra?"
he smiled, "Sort of."
he didn't look to me like he would have an uncle
cool enough for that gig.
"Sort of?"
he looked at me.
"Listen man, Barry just used session men
on all those records. There wasn't really a
Love Unlimited Orchestra.
It was just a name he used on the
record sleeves."

I'd spent half my childhood
imagining what it must have been like
touring with what had to be the best-named
band in the world, and asked myself questions,
would they even fit into one tour bus?
I had always pictured women everywhere
and champagne and polyester
and bras and panties draped over the seats
and now all of it
ruined.

Curtis Hayes

I drove home
opened a beer
and turned on the TV.
two young and impossibly beautiful actors
were quipping cleverly on a park bench
as extras passed by
and a tired classic rock tune
droned through the scene.
I sat back
and let the lies dissolve everything.

Curtis Hayes

Gloomy Sunday

we were in a weekend haze
curtains pulled shut
music warbling around the room.
I hadn't known her very long.
she was a misfit,
a castaway.
she once said, "I obey my own gravity."

her apartment was tiny,
cluttered with shoes, clothes
some old photos and vintage posters.
it was what I imagined
a backstage dressing room in the 1930's
would've looked like.
there was red velvet couch.
there was always music.

Billie Holiday started in with
Gloomy Sunday.
pouring a fresh Gin and Tonic,
I listened to the first verse
and said "Billie Holiday," almost absently.
eyes closed, she slowly nodded her head.
I slid in next to her,
"Do you know the story
about this being the Rumanian suicide song?"
she kept still
balancing her glass on her lap.

Curtis Hayes

I continued,
"Supposedly a bunch of people in Europe
killed themselves
when they heard the original version.
Different lyrics, though."
she kept her eyes closed
we listened as the song crept slowly
into the dark corners of the room.
She took my hand.
"It was Hungary. It was the depression.
Nazis and famine were waiting behind
every streetlight.
That's what did it.
That more than some odd music scales."
there were books scattered around the floor.
the music moved through its minor-keys
and peculiar breaks,
then faded into the upbeat piano sway
of I Wished on the Moon.

there was food somewhere in the kitchen,
there was liquor.
the curtains were thick
and we wouldn't have to think about
responsibilities
or the burn of daybreak
for another eighteen hours.
It was a perfect Sunday.

Curtis Hayes

The Strawberry Field

we hiked through the strawberry field at dusk.
up ahead was a four screen Drive-In theater.
when we were close enough
we unfolded our low beach chairs
and my friend Steven
worked the knobs of a transistor radio
searching for the low frequency
soundtrack feed
beaming out from the projection shack.
our parents weren't interested in
seeing anything about an alien
that hunts and kills a whole
spaceship crew
but all the kids at school were
talking about a scene
where the creature bursts out
of someone's chest
in a fountain of blood.
we had to see that.
Steven found the sound
and set down the radio
in the soil between us.
he pulled out binoculars
from a leather case.
they had belonged to his father
who like mine
was off somewhere
with a new wife
and a new life.

Curtis Hayes

I had a palm-sized brass case
that spilt open into mini opera glasses.
we pressed the optics to our eyes
and listened to the opening score.
there was still daylight lingering
and the images on the screen were unclear.
"These opera glasses are pretty shitty."
I looked around the empty field.
"You think some farmer is gonna kick us out?"
Steven looked around.
"I don't think anyone's around."
he held out his binoculars.
"Let's just trade off every few minutes."

we sipped warm Pepsi
and ate chicken legs wrapped in foil.
a slight breeze cooled the summer air.

the alien popped out of the astronaut's chest.
I only saw a distant white room and a spray of red
while panic stammered into my ears
from the small radio.
it seemed like every time the alien appeared
I was stuck with the opera glasses.
Steven would watch a few seconds and then
generously hand over the more powerful binoculars
but by the time my eyes adjusted
the monster was gone.

Curtis Hayes

"Man it's really creepy looking," he'd say
as I watched terrified crew members
react to whatever I had just missed.
I finally just closed my eyes
and let the radio tell me the story.

when it was over
we folded up the chairs
and walked the mile back to his house.
his mother would soon be forced to move
them away to a lesser life
and we would lose touch.
it would be years before I finally
saw the movie clearly.

one day my phone rang.
it was Steven's younger brother.
my friend was gone.
he woke up one morning and couldn't move his leg.
four months later cancer took him at age 34.
we hadn't spoken in years.
he had a wife and a kid
and I knew he was a better person than I would ever be.

Curtis Hayes

Steve, I know you can't hear me
but I miss you, man.
I wish that we could see all the hidden things
that patiently wait to bring us down.
and not that it matters,
but that night behind the Drive-In
was the finest cinema experience
I've ever had.
sometimes as I drive past a strawberry field
I look for a couple of kids sitting in beach chairs.
I imagine them peering through binoculars
trying to look further out
than our human eyes
will ever be able to see.

Steven Hendrix

I can taste the ash
                this time
it has taken up residence
                on my tongue
found shelter
                in my nostrils
set up camp
                in my lungs

it bore witness to the destruction
the lives lost
the lives that need to be rebuilt
I carry their sadness with me

Steven Hendrix

Prima Facie

Why are you taking me, he said?
With a look of anguish on his face
Like Munch captured in The Scream.
The stone is in your hand, they said.
But I merely picked up the stone,
He said, after it struck me.

Steven Hendrix

Expect Delays

Traveling south on the 405
approaching Seal Beach Blvd
around midnight on a day
mostly forgettable
I see a flashing sign
that warns me to expect delays
as if on cue
all the cars in front of me
stop
and I slam on the breaks
because I didn't expect this

I squint
the lights blend together
in a luminous sea of red

red is anger
     red is passion
          red is danger

I'm almost forty years old
and I'm not a poet
yet
my novel has gone through
starts and stops
     starts and stops
          starts and stops
with no end in sight
yet

Steven Hendrix

my wife moved four hundred miles away
to a city whose gravitational pull
on my heart keeps me in orbit
with nowhere to safely land
yet
I have no children
yet
but I've already prepared
to mourn their loss
while I've tried for nearly ten years
to mourn the loss of an uncle
but I haven't figured out how
yet
and yet. . . and yet. . . and yet

if I had expected this
would it have turned out differently?

I exit the freeway
because I have no patience
for delays
I take the longer route
to keep moving
moving. . . moving. . . moving. . .

Pacific Coast Highway
is like a depleted mine
on nights like these
and the sordid heat
of what would be spring

Steven Hendrix

in most places beyond California
stifles even at this late hour
my movement is audible
as I speed along the uneven road
generating my own wind
which crashes violently
against the windows of the car
until a red light at Warner Ave
forces me to stop again

I turn right at the Jack-in-the-Box
to keep from remaining idle
but it's a dead end
I park in the empty lot
run to Bolsa Chica State Beach
stumble across the sand
because it's hard to walk on
with shoes
I can't see the waves
but I know they're there
because I can hear them

roaring and shhhh'shing
    roaring and shhhh'shing
        roaring and shhhh'shing

like an ancient clock keeping time
but not counting the seconds
or minutes or hours or days
or months or years or decades

Steven Hendrix

or centuries or millennia or ages
or epochs or eras or eons

what is time made of, after all?

I look up at the sky
the moon is red

red is love
    red is joy
        red is happiness

I've never seen a red moon
and I wonder if it has been red before
if I've passed below without noticing
if it even matters
what color the moon is

my balance in the sand
becomes less stable
though I'm not moving
the sound of the waves
becomes louder and louder
the hue surrounding the moon
becomes redder and redder
until a cloud passes over
and it disappears
all is black for a moment
and I'm only moving
with the earth
hurtling through space
at speeds I cannot feel

Steven Hendrix

The First Time Again

The sea gulls spread their wings
    and glided like kites
        against the hard winds

that night on the pier
    in Newport
        where we reintroduced ourselves

and it felt like another first date
and we held hands for the first time again
and we allowed ourselves to dream
        of a future together again

that's the night I remember
your hair smelling like kelp
and your hand feeling soft as sand
and your lips tasting like salt

and that's how I want to remember you always

Betsy Mars

I was texting
    after Coffee Break by Kwame Dawes

After your breakfast and a shave,
bathed and massaged, you relaxed.

The intake person had come –
you hadn't been in hospice
more than 18 hours.
The dietician stopped by
to find out your favorite foods –
no holds barred now that death was near.
The social worker came to offer whatever
other comforts she could bring.

I muted my phone. After all of these visits
and messages from friends and family,
I focused on you at last.
Your eyes were closed
but you were awake, I could tell.

The thing to do was to read you a story,
just as you had so often done.

I don't recall the book,
but as I told you the backstory
and resumed on the page where I had left off,
that damned prescription came to mind.
I said *I'll be right back*, and picked up my phone.
By the time I finished, you had gone home.

Betsy Mars

Letter to a Shipwreck

Obrigado my beached ship, minha amiga.
I am sorry you went down before delivering the loot.
I hope there was no life lost. Or party favors sullied.
I know you were carrying my birthday present—
the one I dropped long ago at 5 years old
(or possibly 6) in the streets of Rio--
the one that made up for the limbless beggars
and for the grassy knoll,
innocence flying away with the bird kites,
soaring.
Where is the walking My Size doll that was promised?
Where is the heart-shaped amethyst with its magic
clear purple protective powers?
Where is the white chocolate, in all its oxymoronic glory?
Where are the window stickers illuminating
brightly, like leaded glass gospel,
heaving?
Meu gato morreu. My bird has flown.
I am sure my ice cream cake has melted
in its confusion: Is it cake or is it ice cream?
and seeped through the hull,
running in delicious fingers to stroke the Amazon
where the piranha wait,
tasting the remains.

Betsy Mars

Morgue-hardened

Once you've worked in a morgue,
smelled the putrid scents,
 inhaled the exhales of dead flesh
and stomach contents, opened
mouths clamped in rigor mortis
and closed unseeing eyes,
can you be light? Can you illuminate
the cause and time of death?
Each blue body your future,
confronting and affronting your nostrils
and dreams. A cold slap in the face of denial,
and anger, and all those other
stages of grief which are just
stepping stones to acceptance,
as the world empties of the ones you love.

Betsy Mars

Premonition of Descent

One last whiff as you linger –
a scent-suspended moment
as the bottle of your cologne shatters.

The glass and your hopes
were brittle when falling
from the safe ledge
of the medicine cabinet,
from the ledge of your marriage,

by some inner movement
that made you finally
take that leap

of faith that you promised me once
before your nerve failed,
the faith promised a third time

until death do you part
was the only way out
of the life
or the trap, the trappings.

The liquid flowed down the sink,
released at last,
irreplaceable and finite,
your spirit evaporated.

Like a bloodhound, my nostrils flare
on the quick-fading trail
that you followed,
will shattered, two weeks later.

Lee Anne McIlroy

California Summer 2018

Mars casts a single evil eye
Blood red, flinching and near
Like a single ember in a charcoal heap sky
The trees are silver now
Pewter snow drifts down from a furnace cloud
Smoky ghosts float through a sherbet miasma
The deer and the raccoons flee
As glowing, angry fingertips try to catch them
We fill buckets of water
And wait for the first earthquake

Lee Anne McIlroy

Memories of Eldorado

It is the airplanes I will remember most
How closely they flew just above The Forum
That giant red and white lotus
Floating atop a cement pond
I will remember how the planes seemed to hang there and hover
Like birds of prey
Silent and still
Looming, staring, waiting
I will not think about what we destroyed here
When the tide carries me back
Back out to sea, back home
The way we came
But in reverse
Past Avalon, following the coast southward
Along the Cape where the wind feels like daggers
Then north again and across the sea
Back through time
Until I am home again in Cadíz, where the pomelos are the size
Of human heads
Then I will remember the planes
How they glimmered from afar
How the sky was full
Of sunshine and shadow
And shining, floating, shimmering orbs of gold

Kathryn McMurray

Civilization

I was a beast child.
Feral rage-cry ripped my gut open,
Unleashed by some deep old sister
Lodged somewhere in my juvenile spine.
Do not come near, said my wild eyes.
I fought you off, you and your arms,
With tooth, nail, open-palm slap,
With fierce little pinch and hot spit.
I bent your ring finger back.

I don't know why I was mad now.
I was eight, maybe nine.
But it felt good to let it out—
That murder in my blood.
I had Cain's rock held over a head.
A foot on someone's throat.

But you trapped me in your arm,
A brutal scoop, a wrestling move that stilled
The fiend in me. Your fingers seemed to snap
Shut, and no matter my twists and screams,
You held me fast, tight,
Though I whipped my hair in your face,
Cursed, sweat, vowed to run away
The second you let go.
But you didn't. You locked your grip.

Mother, how long did that gruff hug last?
How long did you hold your wild child
Until she surrendered her burden?
How long did it take to make me a person?

Kathryn McMurray

Buddy
for my dear friend Tony

Today I kissed my friend on the forehead and said goodbye.
I called him "buddy," like I call my son so many times each
    day
that I cannot count. I said, *Goodbye, buddy. Hang in there.*
I cringed when the words tumbled stupidly out, too late to take
    back.
This man I called "buddy"; this man, who used to want my
    body
when we were in our twenties, and drinking and talking
about the particular genius of The Beach Boys; this man, who
    is dying;
this man, who you always said looked like a leprechaun
because of his silly facial hair and plaid pants.
What comforting word can you say to that person who,
like a mean older brother, punched you in the arm, told you to
    buck up, chuck?
How do you soothe a man who rated your bad boyfriends,
guffawed at your dumb outfit and wrote a song with your
    name in it?
You call him "buddy" and kiss his forehead.
That's how.

I cried as I went out the door, knowing that I was headed for
    three-year-old energy,
breastfeeding and a dirty house, knowing that the car ride
back home was all I would get for grieving this night:
ten minutes. What a strange, short drive;
desperately unremarkable, tragically boring.

Kathryn McMurray

I pull into the driveway and they are waving from the window.
My sons have pressed their noses to the glass. Children are
    ruthless in their desire.
They don't care who's dying. They want you; that is that.

I tickled everyone to bed; I read the stories they wanted;
Everyone got fed and bathed. I heard myself each time I said,
"*Buddy*, put those PJs on," or "*Buddy*, it's time to get in bed,"
and winced a little at the sound of it.
The moves I made, the things I said, reminded me
of all the forehead kisses, the winks and snuggles, the hair
    tousles,
the touch we need at the start, and at the end.

Kathryn McMurray

Jonah Brushing His Hair

At six, he's just realized that he can make choices about his
 hair,
that there's this other way of being around in the world.
He's got mirrors cocked at angles to comb through the
 possibilities.
Step stool pushed to the running sink, he wets the brush and
 smoothes it through, front to back—
I'm thinking, Wall Street man, 80's yuppie. I can see myself,
reflected, standing in the corner, watching him try this out.
Next, he goes for a mid-1800's banker: split down the middle,
slicked down the sides. He smiles at my watching without
 looking
directly at me. I get smaller and smaller, recede into tininess,
 obscurity,
a smudge in the corner of an otherwise clean mirror.
I smile an infinite and disappearing smile back
as he becomes a toothless Clark Gable, a 50's rough after a
 bar fight
smoothing his hair back into place with his pocket comb.
This may be my last chance to watch my son brush his hair.
I'm a dot. I'm a speck. I'm a memory
of his mother watching
him brush his hair.

Kathryn McMurray

In the Dirt and Dead Leaves

My cat Lola is dragging her hind legs across the back porch.
Her legs are limp, and she strains against her own weight,
pulling herself little by little across the concrete.
Because she can no longer clean herself properly,
her grey calico fur is matted all along her back.
She wants to be alone in the dirt and dead leaves.

Twenty years ago, she fit in the palm of my hand.
She liked to nap inside my dirty running shoes back then.
No matter how many overpriced pet beds I brought home,
Lola always curled up in the dirt, in the dust, in the dark.
She did not grow into a loving or pretty cat.
We had to warn visitors not to pet.

I got the feeling that Lola waited all day, every day,
to escape, and she took every chance she got.
When she got out, I spent hours calling,
in the night or in the day, down alleys, yelling into crawl spaces,
leaving open cans of food at the back door,
cooing "Here Kitty, Kitty!" into the moldy darkness
beneath the apartment building.
Sometimes she'd be gone for days.
She never came back willingly. I pulled her,
hissing, yowling, by the paws, by the tail
out of the grime, covered in cobwebs, eyes wild.

Kathryn McMurray

When I pick her up, she is light and she doesn't fight.
Her legs dangle uselessly, no kicking or scratching.
She doesn't make a noise. She closes and opens her eyes.
Across the patio is a cushion, a bowl of water, food.
I set her down. I move slow, gentle.
On her cushion, I stroke above her nose.
But now she's moving, dragging herself away again.
She's using all the energy she's got.
Maybe for the last time, maybe not.
She's headed for the dirt and the dead leaves.
That's where she wants to be.

Karie McNeley

The Beggar Becomes Chewser

She stalks the boulevard,
hungry, holding a paper plate
in her mouth like she used to
in the tumbled roads of Joshua Tree.
Salivating while small dogs bark
from homes beyond the sidewalks
and cats wander atop brick walls,
trailing long-tailed paths of prey
behind them as they search
for birds.

The coyote feels it's stomach ache
in anticipation. Starving for flesh.
For something to ease its bloodied
bite of pain.

Are you the coyote? I've seen you tumbling in the dirt
asking strangers for money with a McDonald's
cup in hand on a whizzing corner
of 4th street.

Are you the coyote leaping every fence
and flipping every lid only to get
the scrapings from a
discarded paper
plate?

Why do you continue to fault the constellations
guiding your path as you and the coyote
howl together, bellies full of the neighbor's
cat-eyed Moonlight?

Karie McNeley

You broke mom's finger like a chew toy.
Fractured bones and a river of sorrow,
with one gnarled and swift bite
Last Saturday. And I can't
put my finger on it. Brother,
are YOU the coyote?
Howling for a payout
of flesh?

Are you really begging to choose,
or are you choosing
to beg?

Karie McNeley

Reciprocate and Replicate

This failure-feigned heart
lies latent in your doorway.
Knuckles bruised from knocking
hard-headed oak for months.

No reply.

All these star-spangled attempts
to bring back a doomed-future fate;
a faded handwritten message
scrawled in tired, trembling black ink
shoved into an overstuffed mailbox.

No reply.

Remnants of history, gone soon
along with the walls and the roof,
but I'll hold close to toppled shambles
of discarded bookshelves I've turned into art.

No reply.

Gearing up for extremities memories
to mark like scars, permanent derailment
of thought, trapped inside a thought,
and another. A riddle of heart and soul
memorialized on a shaken Etch-A-Sketch.

No reply.

And somehow hindsight still goes wild and strong
from this padded room with painted view.
An absence of frame makes it easy to reign,
reciprocate, and replicate so many visions of you.

Karie McNeley

Ford Flex

She said she could see
a small sliver of road gangster
peering out from underneath
my slacked collar
and buttoned sleeves.
I confirmed.
I was transforming,
and letting my insides out
one slice of swagger at a time,
flipping the faulty pigeons of my past
like quarters
and only accepting the coins
that land on tails.
Bald eagles.
Because I've been stuck
in heads,
my own and others,
for years.
And I no longer need the perception
of a dead president
to hold me back.
I've been walking on two legs
for too long,
missing out on action,
wallowing like a woodpecker
in a forest with no trees
while I could have been flying on four wheels
and flexible,
and free.
Ringing in the new year
with a fresh smile, wind in my hair,
and feathered wings that glide
for miles among the clouds
of beautiful
black
roads.

Penelope Moffet

Balcony

After a year the delicate basil
is stripped of its leaves overnight:

two fat green caterpillars
arched on the stems.

Cherry tomato that offered only
sour fruit in summer

fills with red sweetness
now that it's cold.

Why do I bother
fretting the future?

Penelope Moffet

Landline

I'm going back to the 20th century
on a phone as red as a firetruck,
a cherry orchard, apple of my ear
hooked to a landline
and a small white box
on the green bartop
as physical as you or me,
not an anonymous
slot on the AT&T.
You thought it
hard to reach me
in my cell
on the cell
frequently turned off
to guard against
those gamma rays.
Just try me now.
Even mornings
when the ringer's mute
on the flame-red rotary
in the apartment's heart
the whirring
of the answering machine
will tell me
someone wants to sing
into my ear
like the golden
open-beaked
canary
stickered
to the center
of the dial.

Penelope Moffet

I've been amorphous
long enough. Time
to resume shape
and color, locate
others of my species,
send electric roots on down.

Penelope Moffet

Highwire

Nothing seems to hold the crossbeams up
except one lousy ledge the foot of one
depends on and a vertical board the other
half-leans on above the wall that splits
the room. Otherwise these two-by-fours
are on their own. They cross in mid-air
to suspend a burnt-out globe above
room's middle and a klieglight right above
the john. Any quake should bring these down
but they've outlasted major shocks
though the fountain in the backyard ruptured
in the last big earthgrowl and the bricks that line
both yards are all askew. Cobwebs drape the beams.
Housekeeping is casual here,
as casual as the housebuilding that planned the joists'
suspension of belief, suspension in belief
nothing big enough to knock them down
will come along. A lot depends on Faith,
Faith and Denial, schizoid girls
who improvised this thin-skinned shell
into a home. Don't even ask about the way
the woodstove's pipe cuts through the roof.

Penelope Moffet

**Couplets Written in the Dark
In Search of Home**

Never to leave home again
Never to face sorrow

In the light, dark water carving
Through a snowy field

In the dark, a cocoon
Hung in space

Couplets written in the dark
Couplets written in the dark

Green light of the ceiling smoke alarm
So steady, then it flicks out red

Tip of an airplane wing
Charging through the dark

White noise of the fan I don't turn off
Making moving forward in the dark

Couplets written in the dark
Couplets written in the dark

Couplets written in the dark
In search of home

Zack Nelson-Lopiccolo

old crows

two crows walk into a bar
one wing stretched out asking for a bourbon
the bartender only nods and slides a box
full of Belgian brandy begging
to be drank on a boggy
shore in some pub called Beirut
the second crow screams midnight bursts
at a fellow patron before banging
his head into a red bottle of burgundy
and suddenly remembers he wants a baguette

Zack Nelson-Lopiccolo

-- -- .. -- -- -- -- -- -- -- . . . . (Morse code "Zombies")

Existence has presented itself
but no longer cares. No one
acknowledges the actuality of life,
hard facts that crack
on the head like a baseball bat
in a 7-Eleven parking lot at four AM
off of South St. in north Long Beach.
Presence has become reality television,
and quit dancing with the night stars
to join the burn of celluloid in living rooms
thousands of miles, yards, feet apart,
interrupted from speech by voiceless
transmissions, nothing but dashes and dots
in Morse text messages.

Zack Nelson-Lopiccolo

Sleep
    After Jack Grapes

Sleep is a stabbed animal
bleeding across the carpet.
Its violence shatters glass
and keeps us in love.
A capital "L" because
this shit ain't easy.
Because ain't isn't a word,
but a conjunction for slang.
Our everyday vernacular
that ends with one of us
saying a sentence in the wrong
tone, stumbling over simple words.
After all we will dress the stabbed
animal, lay it in a pan smothered
in oil and herbs, bbq it and forgive
ourselves in the constant
choke and poke of partnership.

Zack Nelson-Lopiccolo

Charlie Parker

It keeps happening, this dream
about umbrellas. The scene
always different, but the song
constantly the same,
Charlie Parker's Ballade.

Every night thousands march
down a street lined in high
rises without owners. The song
reverberates off the concrete
the streets are scuffed and covered
in gum and newspapers.

Billboards are covered in black dots
dribbled down like dying dogs
wet and withered into shriveled
carcasses. And it's here underneath
the empty boards, hanging on
a ladder covered in paint

eyes bloodshot, a bottle of Maker's
Mark in one hand and a handkerchief
in the other, that I fall, and fall, and fall
into endless piles of umbrellas
heaped forty stories high.
And there's never a way out.

Shannon Phillips

May Crowning
for Sarah

Morning is for many things,
one of them: roses.

On this morning, the sun rose
but there is no sunlight,

only gray. Light rain
may grace the rose,

but our hands

our hands only cut
what our eyes chose.

Shannon Phillips

Grandma's House

I don't remember the door,
but I remember the delicate
ribbon of dark green mold
wrapped around the throat
of the home's foundation.

I also remember the ornate frames
of paintings—so many paintings,
the eye couldn't rest—dusted
with metallics, a nightmare to dust.

The coffee table—a block with claws
—like the heavy drapes, the thick
upholstery—not dirty, not clean

until a few drops of peroxide
escaped from a cut,
and a child's eager wipe
upon watching the wood surface
go from dark to light.

Shannon Phillips

Landscape Photographer Wanted
for James

Under his eye, the line
of her body becomes
a horizon.

He follows it, as far
as the light will allow;
No one is greater
than the sun.

At night, under
his hands,
she is infinite.

No one is more
loving than the moon,
who gifts us with shadows
and tether.

Wendy Rainey

Melania

We want to feel sorry for you
because your husband cheats on you
with strippers
and Russian prostitutes.
We suspect that your son has a disability,
and that you are abused, terrified,
and being held captive by a fascist dictator.
Give us a signal –
something bolder than the usual recoiling of your hand
from his,
and we'll send in the Marines
or Tom Cruise.
Melania,
we want to get comedians fired
and ruined for life
to save you and your son
from ever being the butt
of anybody's joke.
We saw by the way you eschewed heavy makeup
and expensive clothes
at the toddler internment camp
that you were deeply affected
by the Honduran children screaming for their mothers.
Oh, Melania,
a woman we are told, speaks five languages,
a woman with impeccable fashion sense.

Wendy Rainey

We know you didn't mean it
when your $39.00 jacket declared,
"I really don't care. Do you?"
Melania, we want to lay down our bodies
in the mud
so that you may walk all over us
in your Louboutin heels.
Maybe you can spear
some of those caged babies
with your stilettos
and kick them
– humanely –
back to the hell they came from.
Melania,
take our social security,
our health care,
the after school music program,
and the food stamps from gramma's cookie jar,
and buy yourself a dozen gold plated G-strings,
Melania,
please know,
we never intentionally ogled your nude breasts
and waxed pudendum on the internet,
but those free-spirited photos just keep popping up.
We can't be expected to look away,
can we?

Wendy Rainey

That Great Big Beautiful Bastard

My father died alone on a Christmas Day
in the ninety degree heat on a bus bench in Las Vegas.
His death certificate read simply cirrhosis of the liver.
I wasn't surprised.
He had been handsome
and even after he married my mother
he had so many girlfriends
that in high school I used to joke
that I was afraid I would accidentally date my own kin.
The day my youngest brother was born he disappeared
only to resurface two weeks later with a wad of cash for my mom.
He threw it on the dining room table,
claiming he had another family to support,
living sixteen miles from us.

It isn't for me to know why or how
my father's head was split open
outside the Honey Bucket Saloon in Reno,
or what he thought about during the fourteen years
he served out a manslaughter conviction
in Nevada State Prison.
It isn't for me to know why he thought it was a good idea
to call me from Nova Scotia on my ninth birthday
when he had promised to be at my party in Long Beach.
He was ecstatic, telling me about the Northern Lights,
and how he would take me to see them someday,
when my mother grabbed the phone from me,
"Go to hell, you prick," she hissed under her breath.

Wendy Rainey

I don't know my father,
but I remember the look on his face
as I jumped off of the kitchen table one morning.
With one hand he scooped me off the linoleum
and held me to his chest.
He stroked my hair as I screamed.
He kissed my nose
and set me down into the sink
to let the cold water wash the blood off my knees,
and the tears off my face.

My father died alone on Christmas day.
The sun was blazing in the December sky.
My father keeled over on a bus bench
and fell to the scorching pavement,
leaving only an empty fifth of Four Roses Whiskey behind.

My father;
that drunk,
that murderer,
that wife beater,
that burned-out womanizing scumbag.

That great big beautiful bastard.

Wendy Rainey

The Feral Children of Los Angeles

A pack of feral children was spotted walking northbound
alongside the 101/Hollywood Freeway in Cahuenga Pass
just after 6:00 a.m.
during the Monday morning commute.
The leader of the pack
appears to be a ten year old girl
travelling with three other children,
ages five, seven, and eight.
The four were seen engaged in a feeding frenzy
just off the Barnham exit
where a big rig operator was sighted
throwing a bag of Big Macs onto the highway.
At 1 p.m. on Tuesday the pack was spotted
outside an oceanfront bistro.
Patrons of the restaurant were traumatized
as the emaciated children foraged in the dumpster,
stuffing their mouths with cider- brined pork chops
and braised beef belly.
Maple bacon chutney sauce
with wild blackberry liqueur
dripped down their chins
and onto their naked bodies
as they danced and howled,
smearing Black Cod Brulee
on their faces and rubbing it in their hair.

Wendy Rainey

Counselors were on hand
for a group of Malibu wives.
One wife stated,
"So, we were walking to our cars after brunch
and we see these filthy children gorging themselves on
    garbage.
I was like, this is some totally edgy shit!
I gotta document this scene for my blog.
But those little savages
wouldn't even stand still for a fuckin' photo."

Animal researchers have noticed
an increase in pack sightings
over the past few weeks.
"We have known for years
about the feral children of Los Angeles.
What we don't know is how many of them there are.
Up until now they have secluded themselves
in the Hollywood Hills and surrounding Santa Monica
    Mountains.
This recent rash of sightings
may have been necessitated by drought conditions.
Some of our research suggests
that the children have been raised by coyotes
which accounts for the child-like howling
that residents have reported hearing at night."

Wendy Rainey

Experts caution that the youths have developed a taste
for four star cuisine.
"But if these children are unable to scavenge the kind of food
they have grown accustomed to
then anyone who routinely dines in restaurants
rated with more than two Michelin Stars
and lives a life of leisure is at risk for attack.
Those who engage in rigorous physical activity
tend to develop muscle and sinew throughout the body
that make their meat tougher," the coroner explained,
"Hence, they are in the low risk group.
A daily workout alone
will not guarantee one's safety," he warned.
"These youngsters have, in a very short time,
cultivated a highly sophisticated palate.
They are on the hunt for soft flesh
that has been marinated in expensive port
and gourmet cuisine."

Bloggers at Winelyfe.com speculate
that when the children taste the flesh of their prey
they are tasting "Hints of Demerol and Vicodin,
lifted by kale juice and coconut water,
steeped in a deep bitter brooding,
characterized by self-indulgence
flirting with regret
and the inability to age gracefully."

Wendy Rainey

Authorities are still investigating
the attack that occurred Wednesday night
as two Pacific Palisades residents
dined on their terrace.
All that was found at the scene
were their leather yoga pants
and a pair of six inch Gucci stilettos.
Their bodies have yet to be recovered.

Steve Ramirez

Dear Wisconsinites

Look at the face of a refugee and try to see yourself.
Think about what you would do if your town was more crater than building.

Imagine reading about boys from the Elks Lodge finding another family
floating under the ice of Lake Michigan, their faces bloated like bluegill.

Picture yourself at the kitchen table, crossing cities off the map
as the names lose their meaning. Marking X's along the highways,
because there's no way to reach Chicago or Minneapolis anymore.

Imagine the worst day of your life.
Tear it from the calendar and wrap it around your shoulders like a blanket.
Wear it while you wait, while your town grows smaller than the graveyard.

Picture your life in terms of paperwork.
How many ways could you prove who you are if you couldn't go home?
What would you do if your bank, your house, your friends didn't exist?

Steve Ramirez

Think about where you'll go when the Red Cross says it can't send help,
when all the hospitals are gone and gunfire sings you to sleep at night.

Imagine hearing the words radical American terrorist & mass shooting
while people talk about you but never speak to you.

Picture opening your mouth to pour your language out,
because nobody else speaks the same way.

Remove your eyes and place them in a stranger's skull.
Look at yourself and tell me what they see.

Steve Ramirez

Letter to an Old Flame: The Upstairs Lounge

i.
We wanted our love illicit: two parts Scarlet, one part Rhett and a hint of a high school Heathcliff in hot pants. We Braille'ed our way into love across the fog-strewn shore of a dance floor, hands and hips murdering our inhibitions one song at a time.

You can't tell my parents, you said as I took you in my mouth. Not the best time to make me laugh.

ii.
My parents found out the same way Columbus discovered America: accidental, irreversible. They didn't find anything new. It's been here the entire time, folks.

No father should walk in on their son, spelunking their best friend's cave, but he should learn to knock. We were still puzzling together these jigsaw bodies. How they fit. How they crash together. How they fall in and out of love like everybody else.

iii.
It's bad enough the wounds were self-inflicted, but the silence...? The laughter...? Our own families carving those names into our foreheads with their eyes. Did it make it easier? Add distance between the men they thought we would become and the disappointment they imagined we were?

Do we ever love a person for who they are, or just paint pictures of them with our minds and hope it's enough?

Steve Ramirez

Somewhere Over the Darkened Curve of the Earth

The ocean holds us together.

Your feet are a compass,
drifting toward my untrue North.

You are the drunken breath of the wind against my lips.

I would fold the world like a map
and take a match to this city
you have forced me to outgrow.

I would burn my way toward you,
but the ocean holds us apart.

My hands are poor excuses for birds,
crawling down the spine of the globe,
blind as the night I birthed them
into this empty house.

The wind says it's time to shush the window closed,
time to sleep this dream to bed,
time to let you go.

Steve Ramirez

Eating A Slug In Germany

I came to the Biergarten searching for something bitter,
like my Teutonic past, or perhaps conversation & Germanic
    bosom,
but instead I found you: soft, slimy minotaur of the night,
all muscle & no shell, no place to call home,
only genetic debris littering your lonely undulations
while you wander this labyrinth of tables & shoes,
mucus trailing behind you, your own ball of string.

After all, aren't you the heart of the puzzle,

stranded in a crypt without a key, doomed by your taste for
    blood,
just as you are undone by your predilection for Pilsner?

We are both tourists here, lured by false promises & cheap
    lager.

You scour the concrete floor, bleary ganglia turning this way
then that, searching for another slug to call your own,
two tiny earthquakes rumbling in the dark,

but instead you found me: an Ausländer in a borrowed coat,
wearing my father's shoes, Theseus with a bellyful of amber
    bock,
surrounded by a half dozen of my cousin's friends, all pale,
    ageless & beautiful
like this town, like the river upon whose banks I will be passed
    out in a few hours,
clinging to the waitress with the smile engineered to ruin
    men's lives,

Steve Ramirez

the buxom blond who speaks more French than I do German,
who is the only reason I'm considering what I'm considering.

They've taken up the chant, fists drumming table tops,
the beer alchemizing this into a rite of passage.

I am supposed to lead them out of the maze,
rescue them from this place they no longer recognize,
a land scarred by the ambitions of our fathers,
the endless hunger of our mothers.

So, little monster, crescent moon, slime-covered Slug of Minos,
I will be your home now.

Kevin Ridgeway

After Hours

a Taj Mahal album crackled from an adjacent
turntable, and i impressed the harmonica player's
girlfriend when i knew the words to
she caught the katy and left me a mule to ride,
every bit as convincing as the voice coming out
of the stereo speaker, that hard headed woman
of mine. the harmonica player's girlfriend
wanted to sleep with me, her head in the kitchen
and her big feets out in the hall. but he put
the kibosh on that especially after i creamed him
at a game of basement billiards and showed
the lead singer up by knowing all the words
to Bob Dylan's Down Along the Cove,
impressing his wife who he immediately
took home with a glare in my direction.
they didn't seem to understand that I was
there for the music, not the groupies.
I guess i shouldn't have kept asking them
to play the same Hank Williams song
over and over and over again.

Kevin Ridgeway

The Eulogists

my older brother and I offer the final words
on behalf of our family
in chapels across the American southwest
the preachers always tactful when they dismiss
the lack of God in our lives
as they launched into sermons.
my older brother was oftentimes the better
received out of the two of our final tributes,
no one got it better than when he said
"without my grandma, I am nothing!"
which was a reel to reel tearjerker favorite,
but many would argue that I stole the show
at our mother's funeral by making silly stoner
jokes and reading poems the minister wanted
to preach for alongside the acceptance of
Jesus Christ in our lives.
We have since retired the act, unlikely
to reform our powers of saying goodbye
with praise and the laughing exasperation
in our weary courage to move forward.

Kevin Ridgeway

Batboy Escapes!

read the headline above
the black and white fangs
of a displaced upside down junior cave dweller
trapped by the government for top secret experiments
that were denounced by the Federation of Bearded Ladies
as cruel and unusual, and my mother said no when I asked
her if we could pretty please with sugar throw it on top of
the cat litter, pork chops, artichoke and other groceries
nudging along the supermarket checkstand conveyor belt
that she tossed a celebrity gossip rag full of lies on instead.

Kevin Ridgeway

Cheshire Cat

His role in the play came late in the game,
and he was a revelatory mystery in a flat cap and stripes,
    standing in the shadows beneath a
talking set piece painted to resemble the Cheshire Cat, who
    he gave a beatnik voice to and from
that performance on he was a renegade who stole every
    show, no longer uncomfortable exposing
his bodily instrument and the endless twists and turns of his
    emotional psyche as he sharpened
his craft into a revolutionary trajectory into the wonderlands
    hidden in a cruel world he helps
people escape from, confront, laugh at and maintain a
    righteous hope for, a cat who I followed
down the rabbit hole where it was nearly off with my head, the
    same head with eyes glued to the
dim spotlights at a brother who placed many of my wildest
    dreams within reach like a
supernatural cat in a hallucinatory world full of revelations like
    him on that stage where he found
the dreams he had
always been searching for and he was the first in our DNA to
    rise above a fear to break free of
the silence which killed the rest of our family.

Tere Sievers

Condolence Card

Two red fuchsias in paper cutouts
hang from a branch
on the front of this card,
like ballerinas, bending at the waist.
Inside, the message sent is brief,
Dearest, so sorry, much love.
Is there anything more to say?
I remember John, who came
to our house after Kathleen died.
I don't remember his words.
He wasn't a close friend
but his vigil was a comfort.
The card on the mantle is a comfort,
the fuchsias keep me company.

Tere Sievers

On the Way to JFK
> *The great ones regard every moment like this...*
> *Ellen Bass*

The Belt Parkway is jammed. The cabbie and I chat.
He's from Spain, lives in Jersey, married, 40 years.
I lived in Jersey before California, 50 years ago.
We talk about the weather, spring with cold wind and
spitting rain, our grandkids, the Jersey towns we know.
We talk about traffic as we cross the Verrazano bridge.

He says, *I enjoy every day now. Sometimes, it takes*
two hours from Newark into the City, the tunnels
slow, the weather bad. I just enjoy every ride.
They are always different, the rides, the people.
I watch the families walking. I take it easy, life is short.
It's warm today, the sun shines. The big tankers
sail into the Narrows. I drive the taxi, enjoy the view.

Tere Sievers

His Armor

Framed by white pillows
my father's face is pale.
Foggy after surgery,
mouth slack, eyes closed,
his fingers tap his cheek.
His body looks small,
shows no sign of the anger
he carries like a weapon,
holds like a shield,
wears like a mask.
The nurse lifts the blanket
that covers his bare chest.
Tender without his shield,
I see a spot worn raw
right above his heart.

Tere Sievers

Off the Trail in Joshua Tree

On the main road, too many cars.
I slow down, pull into a sandy spot,
get out and walk into the scrub.
I see nothing but rocks and the distant
bouldering hills, all tan and gray,
color-bleached by mid-day sun.
Eyes looking up, I trip and slide,
fall into small rocks: red, shiny, black.
For a minute I am still, turn my head.
By me, a tiny garden of wildflowers,
the blossoms shaped like trumpets,
wheels and cups, all bee-decorated.
An ant finds my foot and bites.
I am in the desert now.

Francesca Terzano

The Death in the Large Family: Part 1
For Michael Mannor

He overdosed.
On what?
Heroin.
Did he always have a drug problem?
Not till he got older—he was an artist and played music. Do you remember him?
Not really—he wasn't my generation of cousins.
He lived with Grandma and us, you got to live with mom.
At least Grandma took you all in.
Two Weeks Later—
It wasn't heroin.
What was it?
Opioids.
That's what heroin is.
No, medical opioids.
Oh, but he still OD?
Well yeah, but it's suspicious.
What do you mean?
The carpet they found him on was cleaned by bleach.
Two Months later—
Will you come?
Mom, I didn't really know him.
Your sisters aren't—
Okay, I'll come.
Later That Night—
I'm going to my cousin's funeral tomorrow.
That took a while. Hasn't it been two months?
I don't know the whole story, but he died suspiciously.
Do you want me to go?
No, you have work.

Francesca Terzano

Today—
>We arrive at 1:57.
>Three minutes early.
>A cousin I only recognize from her tattoo I've seen on Facebook comes up and hugs me, and the others I've only seen as children do the same.
>I hate hugging strangers, but since they are family, I give in.
>Finally, cousins arrive I know.
>They get big hugs.
>I wonder why someone dying is what brought us together.
>A funeral was the reason why this many family members were together before.
>Grandma's funeral twenty years ago.
>*Where's your sisters?*
>*One's on the east coast, and the other one refused to come. She doesn't go to funerals. She didn't even go to Grandma's remember?*
>*Oh yeah—*
>My mom says hi to my aunt. They hug, and I overhear what they are saying.
>*It was someone in his building I know it..*
>*I though he OD?*
>*He did, but they found bruises on his ribs like someone beat him up, and the cops determined that where they found his body wasn't where he died. They were handing out crime scene photos. I don't know why they would do that, it's illegal if you're not a cop.*
>*Why did they kill him?*
>*He matched the description of someone who raped a girl in the same building, only because he has curly hair*

and a beard, but—it wasn't him—they just targeted him.

My mom hugs, and she says they will talk after the burial.

During the reception they play his favorite song "I Can See Clearly Now" as he is lowered into the grave. His mother starts crying.

My baby boy! My baby!

I think to myself as tears fill my eyes, *why must parents bury their children?*

The pastor asks if we would like to put dirt on his grave. I know it is not my place because I didn't know him, I am agnostic.

But I remember my sisters telling me they were close to him.

I stand up and grab two roses for them, and then a pile of dirt.

I drop the roses into the grave then the dirt.

I am sorry I didn't know you, and that my sisters aren't here.

Later Today—

    While we eat, a cousin I am close to but haven't seen for five years comes up to me,

"You should come down and visit me at my place. It is a total art town, you would love it."

I smile at him. "Yeah. I'll do that."

Francesca Terzano

Obituary: The Sequel
　　For Michael Mannor

　　　　Only a month has passed since your funeral.
　　　　I haven't thought much of it,
　　　　you know
　　　　since I did not know you. We might have met
　　　　As children, but my dad was always weird about me
　　　　Seeing my mom's side of the family.
Then it hit me
　　　　When I was watching a TV show.
　　　　A character died.
　　　　Someone wrote a long obituary.
　　　　At the end it said, "he leaves behind one brother."
　　　　I thought of yours, and similar lines
　　　　In your own. All those you left behind.
　　　　One line read,
"And many cousins"
　　　　I realized,
　　　　I only know you through an obituary.
　　　　These two paragraphs that briefly cover your life
　　　　Because you were so young.
　　　　Some gaps were filled by family.
　　　　But all I know is you are Uncle Kurk's kid,
　　　　You played guitar and had curly hair.
People think big families talk to each other.
　　　　But we don't. Over twenty first cousins,
　　　　I only regularly talk to two.
　　　　Even at your funeral when the family talked
　　　　About getting together again,
　　　　I heard one cousin snicker,

Francesca Terzano

"I don't want to do that."
    Even though she just lost you, her brother.
    I can't say that this experience will make me
    Talk to our family.
So, if there is an afterlife.
    Maybe we can all talk there,
    Because Grandma will be there,
    And God only knows how mad she is
    At us for not talking to each other.

Francesca Terzano

Sunshine: Final
  For Michael Mannor

This is the last one, I promise.
I was picking up my sister from the airport,
And remember the song playing at your funeral.
"I can see clearly now the rain is gone."
But I still have no memories of you.
My sister explained
Why she couldn't come to your funeral.
She thought it was going to be in Ohio,
Where you lived, and she was.
She told a different story from your mom.
You were in fact a drug addict,
But not heroin.
Don't worry, I'm not here to judge.
I'm just happy that you are free
From your addiction.
She said you wanted to live on the streets.
That you shaved your beard the night before.
You fell asleep on your brother's couch,
And didn't wake up.
She said that she didn't know why your mom
Was creating rumors
Throughout this big family.

My sister told me more about
The time she lived with you at Grandma's house.
A ranch house.
With a lot of trees and long dirt roads.

Francesca Terzano

Chickens ran free, and dirty dogs loved
To play and chase children.
My sister said you
Ran around without your shirt on
With your brother. When she said this,
My memory saw three boys without
Shirts climbing a tree, telling me to join them.
Because there was a tree house on top.
I was too scared to climb the tree.
I don't know which of the three is you,
But one is.
So, I'll hold on to this little bit of sunshine
And remember that as you.

Sarah Thursday

Fate Ignores My Resolve

When I put these words on the page, they leave
my hands – they take on form, a life outside myself.
Silence is my enemy so I speak you. I write it down
and read you out loud. I refuse to let these moments
fade like sun bleached houses, weathered and
forgotten. I speak you. I speak my story as an
owner of its truth. I have to reach back far behind
me where I left your memory until you shook it out
from the ground. As a decade had passed, I
acknowledged its finality and how I had pulled
myself up and over your demolition of my young
heart. It's wiser now. It never once stepped backwards
towards that girl spellbound by you and your collared
leash around her insecurity. I brushed my dusty hands
and walked so far, I forgot that place. I hardly ever
bothered explaining that old tale why your name
could untie my resolve, upturn this forward motion.
It was past even any lingering whisper that I could
crumble like sun-burnt paper. Fourteen years is
plenty long enough to stop missing you. But Fate
ignored my lack of faith and brought you, of all the
billions of souls in the universe, back to me.
Brought you back to me to retell this tale, to rewrite
the plot, to revise the traits held by these characters
and set a new course, travel a far-off road, and let the
scenes attempt correction. Or so I inaccurately assumed.
Our story has only one ending.

Sarah Thursday

Dreams of Falling

I dream of falling
off cliffs, off bridges
off ladders in the sky
off mile high buildings
always it's the certainty
of my descent
I never used to be
afraid of heights
but now I wake
my here body taunt
my heart, my stomach lurching
forward, back to now
awake even from a slight drift
it's like a punch to my gut
how did I leap out,
how did I slip my hands
it's not the impact
it's the fall, the descent
inability to hold on
to anything, to anyone

Sarah Thursday

Water Witch

The tip of my nose
is sun kissed, the way
he used to kiss me there

So I wash it
I scrub the layers
until the layers are
unrecognizable, the way
my present tense is
peeling off blemishes

So I cover it
with sunscreen and
skin-tone make-up, the way
it protects my skin cells
from harmful UV rays

As I study the lines
across my surface
like paths I've taken
or have yet to take
I have no plan for it

All my cells are drifting
sending forward, the way
dowsers search for water
willow branch bent
divining rod leading out

My nose, I don't know where
the water springs eternal

K. Andrew Turner

For Rosa

She has known me
forever, watched me grow
up during the 80s
90s,
    elementary school smiles
and junior high blues.
And now, grown.

I've known her
forever, too. O

I remember her under
the golden walls of Sergio's,
smiling, watched her laugh
under a plastic parrot,
    in the old building.

I remember her steps
quick
    sure
and the way she laughed
at jokes, old sayings,
ringing up orders, cheerful
in the summer heat.

K. Andrew Turner

They've moved.
    And I've come back,
once I found a job that paid
me well enough. I've indulged myself
in childhood treats
  Friday's after work
  before a vacation
    after a vacation
Sergio's has always been a symbol
  of home because of her.

There, Rosa's smile, friendly,
brightens my week.
      She knows me.
  Sees me.

This is me, saying that I see her, too.

K. Andrew Turner

Atomic Spaces

Wonder
   at the dark
         ness
beyond the light
   the in-between
space   surrounding us all

do they connect?
    or separate?
  make us one?
or many?

With the emptiness
    around
 let us rejoice
at our distinction
   and let us be happy
in our sameness.

K. Andrew Turner

Better Worlds

It would take a lifetime to know
all there is to know about science fiction
a life I cannot dedicate.

But I have studied, dipped my toes
into those fresh pools of far away galaxies,
dined with Ursula Le Guin's Left Hand,
watched ships became laser-fodder,
and admired ghostly technologies.

And each leaves me yearning for more
for a world better
                than the one I am in
where at least there is hope
   that we do not end up our destruction
even though that is
                exactly where we are.

I leave the writers to amass
their holdings, let them decide what is saved
let them build
       and build and build
their worlds up. We do not choose
       rather the future will
and in that distance, I know
we will become one people
with facets and dimension
(as we already are)
       but then
we will know and stop
our senseless destructions.

Final hope of the visionaries
we love, their warnings heeded
and peace our tranquil winnings.

K. Andrew Turner

Amor de Madre
    For the art by Junior Mora

She sits, with paintbrush
in hand, a small child on her lap
in swirls of greens browns pinks reds
and dark blue imagination.
She speaks to life the world.
She curls over him,
protecting with slender arms.
All the beauty
and terror whorls
unbridled around them.
A gift of creativity
she whispers magic
"enchant, enchant"
and breathes life
again.

Susan Vannatta

My Mother's Perfume

Dark Vanilla.
It was always
exactly the same.

It lingered

in hair
in couch pillows
in bedsheets
in between

the world

and me.

It was glass,
a purple bottle.
It was hope
one day
I would be
a Woman.

A purple bottle
dark vanilla
rolling in bedsheets

Woman.

Susan Vannatta

Brian's Late Funeral

Two nights ago I passed your old apartment –
the one you shared with J.P.,
the one next to Cafe Ambrosia
(which is closed, now, and covered in vines
and weeds). It was dark
and the bars hadn't closed yet,
so the street was quiet. It took me a long time
to cry. I could feel the words
in my throat, weaved up into a ball
that I couldn't swallow around. I couldn't say them,
not after all this time. And would you hear me,
anyway? I'm still not sure
if I believe in heaven – and I wasn't sure
if a drunken Monday night was the time to start.
*But if I don't believe in an afterlife, then you
must really be gone, right?*
And that's when I cried. I cried ugly
and loud on the sidewalk. I sunk down
against a brick wall and watched
the black iron gate across from me,
waiting for you to walk out again –
I saw you swing the gate open, smiling in headlights,
I saw you leaning against the tree, talking to Philip,
I saw you running to the corner, calling after J.P.,
I saw you turn to me, watching as I cried in the street –
your ghost faded away as a neighbor
walked through you, and I left
before the stranger could ask me
if I was alright. I turned around once, at the corner
to thank the building
for the funeral I never got to see.

Susan Vannatta

The Desert; a Love in Pictures
for Jessii

In the frayed photos of us you smile,
you are always smiling—frozen
in a flash of *1...2...3!*
There is no photo of our darkness,
only teeth and dimples and lips
pressed to the round pink
of cheeks. There was no camera
on the day your parents found out
what we were, the day we were caught
kissing on the trampoline. I can still feel
the warmth radiating from the black
mesh, the May sun, the curls of your hair
tangled in my fingers. I can hear
the squeak of springs,
the sliding glass door, your father
yelling something about dykes
and disgust. There is no picture
of the night you hit me.
My jaw still aches when I smell
the smoke of too many cigarettes
and pipes trapped in a hot garage
at three a.m., or the must
of an old checked couch.
I can taste the cheap vodka
on my lips (or yours), the blood
from the inside of my cheek

Susan Vannatta

when I tried to tell you
that you'd had enough, the salt
water on the corner of your mouth
where I kissed you
when you were sorry. There is no proof
of our last day together.
No evidence of the water
of the aqueduct running to the right
and two hundred yucca trees
standing still on our left, the burning
of my bare feet on the rocks
and the hot wind whipping
at our backs, your voice,
small and quiet, asking me not to go,
telling me to stay there in Neverland,
where we would love each other
like kids forever, the smell of aloe
and cucumber in your hair,
the taste of the sweat on your shoulder,
the lump of words caught
in the back of my throat, your tongue.
When I left in the morning,
I told you to smile. I counted
1…2…3! I stuck the picture
in my dash, watching your smile
the whole drive down
to L.A. I remember seeing the flash,
hearing the whir of the photo
being spit out, touching the warm
film paper as I shook
the picture to life. I can't remember
if I kissed you goodbye.

Susan Vannatta

Beau

Miles and miles of dirt stretched out before me. Six acres, my grandpa once told me, were his. The next door neighbor had sixty two. Six acres, though, were mine. I ran them like a wild dog. Barefooted, with hot rocks digging into the soles of my feet, rattling beneath me as I kicked off each naked foot. I ran with briars sticking into the sides of my legs. I ran through dry and dying bushes, twigs cracked and scratched at my shins. I ran up over hills and slipped down over cliffs. I ran through thick, hot air. I ran through rattle filled holes and prickled plants. I ran. I ran until my mouth was dry and my tongue was coated in desert dirt dust. Beauregard ran with me. He ran over rocks, through bushes, with briars and rattles and sticks and twigs. He ran until his tongue was coated with desert dirt dust.

Beauregard died that summer. We buried him beneath the dirt and stacked rocks beneath a white wooden cross. Somewhere, Beau runs still. I only walk.

Michelle Thomas has always had a great love of poetry. For many years she was a Library Media Assistant at Long Beach Unified School District sharing her love of reading with a multitude of students.

Kitty Anarchy is an anarchafeminist, chicana womyn poet and short story writer. She has a background in social work having earned her MSW from California State University, Long Beach. She has 7 cats, her favorite being ChiChi and 2 dogs named Bandit and Nibbit. She is published in *Rabid Oak* online literary journal. *www.kittyanarchy.com*

Lloyd David Aquino teaches at Mt. San Antonio College. His new chapbook, *Concrete's Song*, is available through Picture Show Press.

Lorraine Biteranta cares more about her cat and dogs than anything else. All she wants in life is a house big enough to hold as many animals as she wants and a little desk to keep writing - probably about them.

Francesca Borella is a writer and anthropologist, who lives in Riverside, California.

Scott Noon Creley holds an MFA in poetry from California State University, Long Beach, and a BA from UC Riverside. His work has been featured in the collections *Bear Flag Republic, Cadence Collective: Year Two* as well as in quality journals as diverse as *Sentence, Miramar, Spillways, Pravic* and *The Carnival Literary Magazine*. His most recent book *Digging a Hole to the Moon* debuted in the top 50 on Amazon.com's poetry section. He recently returned from China, where he was a featured read for Beijing Normal University, the Lu Xun Literary Institute, and Yunnan University in Kunming. He is the founding chairman of San Gabriel Valley Literature Festival inc., a non-profit literacy foundation

Larry Duncan currently lives in Redondo Beach, CA. His poetry has appeared in *Juked, the Mas Tequila Review, Danse Macabre, the Free State Review* and John Grochalski's *Shipwrecked in Trumpland*. He is the author of two chapbooks, *Crossroads of Stars and White Lightning* and *Drunk on Ophelia*. To learn more about Larry and his writing, visit at *http://larrydunc.wix.com/larry-duncan*.

Barbara Eknoian's work has appeared in *Pearl, Chiron Review*, and *Silver Birch Press*'s anthologies. She was twice-nominated for a Pushcart Prize. Her recent novel, *Susie Once Again* is available at Amazon. She hails from New Jersey and has never lost her accent.

Jeffrey Graessley lives in La Puente, CA. His poetry can be found in several magazines and newspapers. He is currently finishing his senior year at Cal Poly Pomona as an English Literature major with a minor in Writing Studies.

Sarah Gurney is currently a student alumna at Mount San Antonio College in Walnut, California. She lives with her mother in Diamond Bar, California.

Curtis Hayes has worked in sawmills, greasy spoons, and as a grip, gaffer, and set builder in film productions. He's been a truck driver, a boat rigger, a print journalist and a screenwriter. His poetry has been featured in *Chiron Review, Trailer Park Quarterly, Cultural Weekly* and other small presses.

Steven Hendrix was born in Long Beach, CA where he spent three days before being whisked away to Orange County where he was raised. He returned to Long Beach to study comparative literature for ten years at CSULB, eventually earning an M.A. He currently resides in San Francisco with his partner Erin and their son Langston. His work has appeared in *Chiron Review, Askew,* and *Cadence Collective*, among others.

Betsy Mars was born in Connecticut and moved a few times during childhood before landing in Southern California at age 6 (and a half). She spent two formative years in Brazil, where she attended kindergarten. She still knows the Portuguese words for cat, dog, please, and come here. Her father was a professor and her mother was a social worker, so she grew up to be a linguaphile, overly introspective, and a bleeding heart liberal. She loves to hang out with her adult children, friends and animals, travel, and write. Visit her at *https://www.facebook.com/marsbitsandpieces/.*

Lee Anne McIlroy is an Associate Professor of ESL at Cerritos College and an Alumni Ambassador for The United States Department of State's Office of English Language Programs.

Kathryn McMurray earned her M.F.A in Creative Writing from California State University, Long Beach in 2004. She is currently working on a manuscript of her poetry and writes short stories. Her work has been published in *Re(Verb), The Bastille, Livewire, Pearl, Epicenter, Red Rock Review, Nerve Cowboy* and *Spork*. She lives in Long Beach, CA with her two sons, and teacher/musician husband, Shannon.

Karie McNeley is a lover of tumbled words on crumpled pages. She's a payroll clerk by day and a tired cat mom by night. She is inspired by confusing life choices, relationships, and 90s cartoons. She writes when things go wrong and right, but mostly wrong, which is severely limiting because her life is pretty good right now.

Penelope Moffet's poetry has been published in *Natural Bridge, Permafrost, Levure Litteraire, Truthdig, Pearl, The Rise Up Review, The Sow's Ear Poetry Review* and other literary journals. Her poems have also been included in *What Wildness is This: Women Write about the Southwest* (University of Texas Press, 2007) and *Coiled Serpent: Poets Arising from the Cultural Quakes and Shifts of Los Angeles* (Tia Chucha Press, 2016). She is the author of two chapbooks of poetry, *Keeping Still* (Dorland Mountain Arts Colony, 1995) and *It Isn't That They Mean to Kill You* (Arroyo Seco Press, 2018).

Zack Nelson-Lopiccolo is the father of cats, collector of words, facilitator of stanzas, epicurean of cheeses and beers, Doctor of walls, bulwark of nature, and reads and watches too much *Game of Thrones*. And now his watch has ended.

Shannon Phillips is a poet, editor, and Southern California native who is constantly in need of a good stretch. When she is not busy napping with her Russian Blue, she is probably obsessing over something: a remark, a muse, a font. For fun, she photoblogs on Instagram under a pen name.

Wendy Rainey's poetry has been published or is forthcoming in *Trailer Park Quarterly*, *Nerve Cowboy*, *Chiron Review*, and several other journals and anthologies. Her book, *Hollywood Church: Short Stories and Poems*, was published by Vainglory Press in 2015. She is a contributing poetry editor on *Chiron Review*.

Steve Ramirez hosts the weekly reading series, Two Idiots Peddling Poetry. A former member of the Laguna Beach Slam Team, he's also a former organizer of the Orange County Poetry Festival and former member of the Five Penny Poets in Huntington Beach. Publication credits include *Pearl, The Comstock Review, Crate, Aim for the Head* (a zombie anthology) and & *MultiVerse* (a superhero anthology).

Kevin Ridgeway writes in Long Beach, CA. A Pushcart Prize nominee, recent work has appeared in *Slipstream, The American Journal of Poetry, Chiron Review, Lummox* and *Nerve Cowboy*. He is the author of the chapbook *On the Burning Shore* (Arroyo Seco) and seven others, including *A Ludicrous Split* (with poems by Gabriel Ricard, Alien Buddha Press). He is the founder of Dark Heart Press.

Tere Sievers was born in New Jersey. She learned to embrace the subtle seasons of Southern California and set deep roots there after moving to marry her husband fifty years ago, have two daughters and now, grandchildren. She says, "Writing poetry helps me see clearly the joys of a long life and teaches me how to survive its losses. Sometimes, it is a spinning straw into gold experience."
Her poems have appeared in *A Year of Being Here, Nerve Cowboy, Silver Birch Press* and *Pearl*. Her first chapbook, *Striking Distance*, is published by Arroyo Seco Press.

Francesca Terzzano grew up in the Inland Empire where she received her B.A and M.A in English. She also runs a very tiny press, Literary Alchemy Press. She also loves cats.

Sarah Thursday, in addition to writing poetry, co-hosted 2nd Mondays Poetry Party, ran a poetry website called *CadenceCollective.net*, and founded Sadie Girl Press as a way to help publish local and emerging poets and artists. She has been published in many fine journals and anthologies, interviewed by Poetry LA, and received a 2017 Best of the Net nomination for "To the Men who told me my Love was not enough." Her poetry books are available at SadieGirlPress.com. Find and follow her to learn more on *SarahThursday.com*, Facebook, Twitter, or Instagram.

K. Andrew Turner writes queer, literary, and speculative prose and poetry. In 2013, he founded East Jasmine Review — an electronic literary journal. His full-length poetry collection *Heart, Mind, Blood, Skin* is now available from Finishing Line Press. He was a semifinalist for the 2016 Luminaire Award. You can find more at his website: *www.kandrewturner.com*

Susan Vannatta, a 26 year old writer, has been previously published in *The Left Coast Review*, with first place in both Poetry and Autobiography. Susan's first Chapbook, *Whiskey Letters*, was published through Arroyo Seco Press earlier this year. Susan uses her life as inspiration for her work, drawing off of the beauty that comes with inevitable pain. When she is not writing, she enjoys a good book, getting lost in her favorite shows, and cooking for as many people as will let her.

134

Acknowledgements

The First Time I Felt Rain *(Previously published in China via translation)*

Cold Confetti *(Previously published in Vulcan, 2008 & in Carnival)*

Civilization & **Jonah Brushing His Hair** (Previously published in Small Fish Big Pond)

www.ingramcontent.com/pod-product-compliance
Lightning Source LLC
Chambersburg PA
CBHW060157050426
42446CB00013B/2877